Dismissed

Copyright © 2008 Kenneth Ralph Fry
All rights reserved.
ISBN: 1-4196-8855-3
ISBN-13: 978-1419688553
Library of Congress Control Number: 2008900601

Dismissed
A True Story of Injustice in the Heartland

Kenneth Ralph Fry

2008

Dismissed

TABLE OF CONTENTS

Part 1

Chapter 1	Life's to Good	1
Chapter 2	I Should Have Known	5
Chapter 3	The Calm before the Storm	9
Chapter 4	Storm on the Horizon	11
Chapter 5	Hurricane Diane	15
Chapter 6	Eye of the Storm	19
Chapter 7	The rest of the Storm	23
Chapter 8	The Aftermath	27
Chapter 9	Total Incompetence	29

Part 2

Chapter 1	The Injustice Begins	33
Chapter 2	Legal Limbo	35
Chapter 3	Not the Victim	37
Chapter 4	Something Good, a Whole lot Bad	39
Chapter 5	Judge Judy	43
Chapter 6	No Civil Rights	45
Chapter 7	Hollywood	47
Chapter 8	Accomplices Revealed	51
Chapter 9	And It keeps Getting Worst	53

Reference

Davenport Police Report	#0511668	58
Davenport Police Report	#0511942	59
Davenport Police Report	#0512191	60
Davenport Police Report	#0512191	61
Davenport Police Report	#0512417	62
Davenport Police Report	#0512417	63
Scott County Complaint & Affidavit	#FECR279164	64
Davenport Police Report	#0517408	65
Davenport Police Report	#0517408	66
www.iowacourts.state.ia.us	Case Dismissed	67

This book is dedicated to everyone who has been, or will be victimized. My prayers are with you.
✻✻✻

CHAPTER 1

Life's to Good

The sense of relief I felt on the flight from LAX to Midway, was more than from a long journey finally over, it was that things were looking very good indeed. After parting from IPSCO Steel Inc. in October, several opportunities presented themselves; therefore I had some long-term decisions to make. So the ten days my wife Lan and I had just spent at the Anoasis Resort in Long Hi, Viet Nam helped me tremendously, and I must say that a villa on the beach in November is truly paradise.

***

On the career front, the contacts I made through Cal Nguyen, the President of Pacific Law, the firm in Ho Chi Minh City that is handling Lan's immigration paper work, were to prove very good. The plan was to move to Ho Chi Minh City the spring of 2005. HACCP consulting was the goal, and things looked very promising, considering that 2004 started out with Lan not receiving her visa in February, the year was turning out to be truly wonderful.

Adding to the fact I was going to be able to live in Viet Nam until Lan got her green card, my mother and I had made amends after a long estrangement. There was however, an undertone of sadness when everyone was told of the impending move and stay of three years.

Friends and family took the news differently. Jeff, my friend of 30 years, took the news hard, he was very sad that I was going to be gone for what looked like to be years. We had many conversations; they consisted mostly of Jeff reviewing all of the possible scenarios of what could go wrong, and how I would fix it from over there. I went on to explain that Diane Merks, the fiancée of Craig Shellabarger was interested in helping out, and we are in negotiations for the conditions of the final arrangement.

Craig, who had been a friend for 18 years, was happy for many reasons. A couple of them are, I am going to make a lot of money and I will be with my wife.

However, the main reason Craig is ecstatic is, they are going to move their family from the tiny apartment in Walcott to my home in Davenport, in order to house and dog sit. It was quite a good deal for them, because they were now 12 miles closer to the children's school.

Diane, ex-law enforcement, and mother of four, had indicated she was interested in purchasing my home with a court ordered settlement she was expecting. I told her, that when she received it we would let the lawyers work out the details.

Until then the arrangement is house sitting, in addition Diane will receive my 1988 K1500 4 X 4 for managing my accounts beginning the spring of 2005. As it turns out this arraignment personally benefits Craig, because he now has only a twenty minute drive to work at New Era Vineyard and tree farm, which is owed by Jack & Beverly Hull.

Jack & Bev are mutual friends of mine and Craig. Jack is a retired photographer, and Bev is a retired English professor. Now they own and operate New Era Vineyard and Tree Nursery next to Wildcat Den State Park.

***

For over 6 years I thought I had been a close friend of Jacks, spending enjoyable time doing things together, and helped him, as a friend would help a friend. I even helped build the winery, when the people that were hired, did not show up to do their job.

I was working 12 hours a day at the local steel mill, when Jack called, and asked if I would help hang roof trusses, because the crane was on site, and only Craig was there. Craig has worked for Jack for decades, doing many kinds of things, and when Craig needs an extra set of hands I will assist, but mostly I just hang out with Jack and shoot the breeze. So when my friend called, I did not hesitate to go to the aid of a friend in need.

When I told Jack & Bev of the plan to move to Viet Nam, they were stunned by the thought of leaving the USA to go to a communist country to work. Jack was curious as to how I was going to earn a living, and plied me with endless questions about what I was going to do. Bev was happy that Lan and I were going to be together, and seemed very interested in meeting Lan.

During the evening, Jack and I discussed what was going to transpire until I went to Viet Nam; I told him there were only two things I had to do. One was having my birth certificate authenticated through the State

Department. The other was to petition a long-term visa from the Vietnamese embassy in Washington D.C...

Jack broached the subject of me working for him full time, by asking me if I thought the equipment in the Film Arts Photo lab in Bluegrass Iowa could be sold, and what would be the best way. I told him that eBay would be the best choice, and the first step would be to take pictures of the equipment with my digital camera, and then setup an eBay account and auction off what we could.

Jack thought this was an excellent idea, and said that in return for my services, I would receive half of what was sold. And in addition to that, I would receive an hourly rate for helping with work not connected to the sale of the equipment.

I spent the next month taking pictures, moving equipment, taking more pictures, and then processing everything to present on eBay. I also had to setup Jacks computer internet service, and eBay accounts, this process alone took three weeks because Jack kept changing the settings, and then forgetting his password, then locking up the computer with to many commands.

Jack and I also did jobs around the vineyard, which Craig was too busy to do. One of the first things we did was to form up a brick patio for a greenhouse; this took us the better part of a week to complete.

Other jobs we did were; pruning 20 acres grapevines, traveling to a vineyard in southern Illinois for a seminar, and making sausages and jerky from the two deer that Jack harvested that season, the later took almost a month to complete.

***

My mother was so excited about our reconciliation, and the upcoming holiday's. That the fact I was leaving for three years did not sink in until February, when I started to remodel her kitchen in preparation for my departure the end of March.

My brother Michael was concerned that I was taking a huge step into the unknown; I reassured him that I had all of my bases covered, and it was going to turn out all right. Just how wrong I was revealed it's self on June 14 2005.

Time sure flies when you are having fun, the holidays have come and gone, my days have been filled with doing paperwork, mailing paperwork, driving from Davenport to Muscatine every day. I have managed to move the bookcases, computer desk, office furniture, clothes, and bedroom furniture in preparation of my house sitter's arrival February 25th.

I also stored my custom Corvette in the storage unit in Bluegrass Iowa, where it would be out of the way, and safe from the elements. My tools and big equipment (i.e. Lawn tractor, snow blower, portable welder, and tools) will stay in the garage and gardening shed.

The arrangement that will govern the house-sitting is, Craig's son Colin is in charge of the house, and will stay after Craig and Diane move, when Diane receives her settlement.

In return for managing my Northwest Bank and Trust account, Diane will receive my Chevy K1500 4x4. The details of this arrangement are; From this account Diane is to pay my MasterCard bill when it arrived in the mail, and deposit $550 dollars before the first of each month as payment on monies owed to me for the Samsung 46" HDTV, 500 watt Dolby 5.1 stereo, and Whirlpool washing machine totaled at $2700.

February 25th passed without a problem. Craig and Diane were settling in, and thanking me for getting them out of the small apartment, promising me they would take care of everything while I was away.

I moved in with my brother Michael in Muscatine, which is only a couple of blocks from my mother's home. Everything was working out great, and in less than 40 days I would be reunited with my wife. Now my only priority was finishing my mother's kitchen and settling up with Jack.

CHAPTER 2

I Should Have Known

That Sunday night at Jack and Bev's, will live vividly in my memory for the rest of my life. We had just finished a wonderful meal and were talking of when Lan and I would be returning to Iowa. When Jack said, "I suppose you would like some money?" I replied "yes that would be nice." Bev and I continued to discuss when I might be coming back to America, and what did Lan think about me living in Viet Nam.

Jack returned with his checkbook and proceeded to write me a check. When I noticed that it was for $186, I asked Jack if this was a joke. He replied with a straight face, "No, that was $10 an hour." When I inquired about the equipment that was sold from the lab, and half of the proceeds, Jack became very indignant, declaring; "I never said you could have half of everything that was sold!"

Then I inquired about the three solid weeks of making sausage, jerky and making sure he didn't poison Bev, by thinking that he could make jerky from raw pork, he just got angrier, and louder, saying that "he never needed my help". I reminded him of the time he unplugged the freezer that contained 50 lbs. of pork shoulder, and 100 lbs of Halibut, and if I had not come to work, it all would have been ruined. He deigned that it ever occurred, taking my leave before something was said that was hurtful, I bid them farewell.

On the drive from the vineyard to my brother's house in Muscatine, my mind was racing over the fact that Jack had never been my friend. In all fairness he owed me $5000 for services rendered and I really needed that money to make the transition as smooth as possible.

When I told Craig what Jack had done, he laughed, there I was standing in my kitchen with someone whom I thought had been my friend for 18 years, who I trusted with bank accounts and other personal information.

I was in shock, Craig was laughing that I had just been ripped off for thousands of dollars, by someone who had said they were my friend. However, I had other problems to deal with such as where I was going to come up with the cash I thought I was receiving from Jack. My solution was to get a cash advance against my MasterCard as time was running out.

***

March 28, 2004; I sign and date the title to the K1500, and make a bill of sale out to Diane for services. I then receive from Craig $550 for April's payment, the next one is to be deposited before April 30. My last instructions to 22 year old Colin, Craig, and Diane; are "I do not want to sell the house, and when Diane receives her settlement, she start looking for a bigger place, also Colin can stay when they move.". I then ask Diane to drive me to the bank, and then to the airport. As we travel, I review with Diane what she is to do every month. She assured me that all would be taken care of. The trip to Ho Chi Minh City was long and uneventful, however at the end of it was the love of my life so I endured it with good sprits.

As Lan and I settled into our studio apartment preparing to spend the next few years in Viet Nam, life was looking good indeed. We spent the first three weeks making trips to Vung Tao finalizing our marriage paper work, and negotiating the best contract for employment.

The final three were Five-0 corp., Gritti Ltd., and ADEN Services. Five-0 corp. was first to offer a position, Operations Director, and it was only a short term arrangement of one year, but it provided a cash flow buffer, and it also allowed me to finalize negotiations with Gritti Ltd.

So off to work I go every morning, to one of Ho Chi Minh Cities Largest Office Building. The Saigon Trade Center, at 65 Le Loi Blvd, my wife was in heaven. Every day, she came by motorbike to the tower to have lunch with me. She thought it very good to have lunch with husband Ken; if you have ever heard the sing song of how they speak English when they are happy, you will know.

***

May 2nd 2005; I went to the ATM to get money for lunch. At the ATM my heart stopped, the screen said; no funds available, the Northwest Bank account was empty. It should have had $500 in it.

My calls to Diane went unanswered, as did my e-mails. I tried to explain to Lan that something was wrong, and that I would have to return to America. She immediately began crying, and saying that I promised to stay in Viet Nam until she received her green card.

The only comfort I could give her was, I could not leave until May 25th. Because I needed our marriage license translated, and authenticated. If I was returning to the states, I was going to file the I-130 from Iowa, and I needed the paperwork before I left.

The hardest thing I've ever had to do in my life was to leave Lan crying at the Ho Chi Minh international airport, telling her I did not know when I would see her again. The second hardest thing I've had to do is endure the flights from Ho Chi Minh to Moline with a million different scenarios of what went wrong, and if everything was going to be all right.

**

My sister-in-law Lisa met me at the Moline airport, which is only a 15 minute drive from my home in Davenport; during that time I do not think we spoke more than 3 sentences.

When we arrived, nothing seemed out of the ordinary. Craig, Diane, and Colin were outside tending to a garden they had made in the middle of my yard.

When I exited Lisa's van, I could hear Colin yelling that it's Ken. As I approached Craig, I noticed that he did not look up from hoeing the garden. I asked him, "What's up?" He still did not look up, nor did he greet me like a friend who had been gone for 60 days, and was not to be back for years.

He was acting like someone who had been caught in the act of doing something wrong. I told Diane that there was something seriously wrong with the account and I needed all the paperwork she had. The reply I received from Diane was one of hostility, and verbal abuse, accusing me of coming and starting trouble. I stated that I wasn't starting anything, that there was a huge problem, and that I needed to find out what happened would she please calm down, and help me by finding the paper work I needed.

After 30 minutes of looking, Diane finally had some documents together. The entire time she was ranting, and raving that it was not her responsibility to have to deal with this. I reminded her, that she received a 4x4 in exchange for dealing with this issue.

During my review of the bank statements, I noticed there was no deposit in the month of April. I found this quite disturbing because, on April 20th Diane had told me on the phone that she had deposited $1100 in the account on April 15th.

When I questioned Diane; as to where the receipt for the April deposit was. She produced me her checkbook, with a duplicate made out to me for $550. I stated that the agreement was; cash to a teller during business hours with a receipt.

Diane's screaming only intensified in ferocity, I looked at my friend of 18 years and asked him what was going on? His only reply "We paid!" I told him "I am going to the bank and that I would get the bottom of this, now give me the keys to the truck". With Diane screaming; "You're a dead man!" I was handed the keys.

***

It is a 15 minute drive to the Locust Street Branch of Northwest Bank & Trust, what I found chilled me to the core. The account was $900 in the red, and there had been no deposits in April or May. My nightmare was only beginning. The drive from the bank to my home was both the longest and ironically the shortest of all my trips so far.

As we pass each other in front of the boat landing on Concord Avenue, I see two big pair of eyes, I guess me locking up all four tires got their attention, because they stop. I told them the bad news of the bank does not have any record of deposits, and is seriously overdrawn.

Craig just sat there repeating over and over that they paid, Diane was screaming threats. I told them both, that they had until the end of the day to get the canceled check, or I would have to proceed accordingly.

Diane continued her ranting and raving, Craig just sat there trying to be invisible. As I returned to the truck and drove away, the most horrible thought occurred to me, I had broken the most sacred rule. Trust no one; and I trusted someone, and now they had possession of my home.

I returned home, and was surprised that they did not lock me out. Looking around my filthy house, I started making phone calls to the Mortgage Company, and Credit Card Company alerting them to a possible fraud situation, one key thing kept popping into my head, I needed to find any of my mail.

CHAPTER 3

The Calm before the Storm

During my search for mail the phone rang, when I answered it, I was surprised that it was Diane, just as sweet as can be apologizing, and saying that they were on the way to the bank to get a copy of the canceled check, and would I please stay for supper, thinking that there was still an amicable solution to this situation I agreed.

I guess that it was four hours before Craig and Diane returned, with stuff for a cookout, and a story of needing to go back to the bank in the morning, because the bank needed to find the check. I knew this could be true so I gave them the benefit of the doubt and had supper with them.

By six o'clock that night I was wiped out, and I still had a 40 minute drive to my brother Michael's.

9 PM June 1st 2005; I felt a little better after a shower and a nap, I sat down with the bank statements.

They tell an interesting story. No deposits, only withdrawals;

April 29th $128.96 HCMC leaving a balance of $ 501.$$

May 2nd $536.18 mortgage service center, leaving a balance of -36.00

May 3rd 2.10 sales tax for overdraft protection

May 3rd 30.00 NSF Fee Charge, at this point the account is roughly $70 in the red.

***

Things really go really bad when the MasterCard payment posts on May 5th, then the mortgage company double posts the account on May 15th. With a realistic grasp of what had happened, I went to sleep with the mistaken thought that tomorrow when I got the canceled check I will be in the good for $500.

CHAPTER 4

Storm on the Horizon

The next morning was a beautiful Iowa spring day, what I did not see was the category 5 hurricane on the horizon, aimed directly at me. The reception I received from Craig and Diane was quite surprising. I told them of the accounting error, and Diane goes completely crazy. Screaming at the top of her lungs; "that after all they have done for me, to come into their home and threatened them in front of their children."

I looked at my friend of 18 years, and asked what was going on? Craig replied; "there is no canceled check and I was to leave the property immediately". Asking Craig if he really wanted to play it this way? Craig replied; "they checked the law and the property was now theirs and there was nothing I could do about it."

With Diane still screaming in the background, I went outside and punched the tailgate of the truck. I knew I was starting to get very angry, and had to calm down.

Craig and Diane had followed me outside; Diane was screaming that I had damaged her truck. I looked at Craig, and asked him one more time if he knew what he was doing? At this point Craig threw fuel on the fire by telling me that; "I have the keys to your Corvette and transferred the title, and everything is ours, get off the property and don't come back!".

***

Noticing that my license plates were still on the white truck, I asked Craig why the truck had not been transferred back in March. Diane said to Craig; "Don't you remember, we decided not to, so Ken would have something to drive when he came back."

My mind was racing, I was thinking that I could salvage something of the situation, because I knew that the title had not been transferred, and 30 days had elapsed, so I could null and void the signed title and retain possession of the vehicle with no repercussions.

I took Craig by the arm into the garage, so I could talk privately with him. I asked him again; "Do you know what you are doing! Do you really want to plat it this way?" Diane stormed into the garage; pointing her finger in my face, and screaming; "I'm an ex-cop, I know the Mafia, and I am going to have you killed!" She then told Craig to kick my ass and make me leave. Craig just stood there with his arms crossed, looking at the ground mumbling; "We paid."

Diane told me that if I took the truck, she was going to report it to stolen, she then told Craig to get into the car that they were going to work. As they drove away, Diane was still screaming at me; "to get off of their property or she was going to have me killed!"

As I drove off in the truck, my mind was swimming, to much stress. I have to admit that driving distracted is a very real hazard, my first stop was the police radar checkpoint set up on River Drive. I received a speeding ticket for 55 in a 45, I'm glad I still had insurance on this thing.

I made it to the county treasurer without further incident, $30 and 30 minutes later I had clear titles to the truck and Corvette. The next stop was the Davenport Police Department, where I was referred to the Scott County sheriff's civil division. So a trip around the block to the courthouse was in order.

After getting all of the details, Captain Mike Brown informed me that in Iowa, you can only have a house sitter for 30 days. After that they become residents, even if there is a contract, and the only way to make them move was to evict them. I once again explained to Capt. Brown, my fears of being a victim of fraud by my one time friend. Capt. Brown told me that he could not offer a legal advice, but if my paperwork was in order, everything would be fine.

My last stop was the post office to stop my mail from going to the house. I needed to get in front of the situation, and to get back to Muscatine to get debriefed by my family.

※※※

Friday Jun. 3rd; another trip to Davenport, this time to settle up with the bank. The agreement we have come to is, $495 to close the account in good standing. In return; I am to receive documentation, that there were no deposits in April or May. With this mission accomplished, I made the decision to visit Bev and ask her for a small short term loan.

DISMISSED

I met her on the gravel road that runs by their home. We exchanged greetings, and a little information about what was happening. I asked Bev if she could help me financially. Her reply was; that she could not help me out, and that I should talk to Jack. I replied that I was more than a little disappointed with Jack, but that I would go talk him.

Jack and I greeted cordially enough, I asked for moment of his time; so we proceeded into the winery. I tried to explain what was happening, but was cut off by Jack saying that he didn't want to get in the middle of your and Craig's problem.

So I just asked for a loan of $400, he replied that he had given Craig over $1000 for me. I was aghast; I told Jack that I haven't received a penny from Craig in over 60 days. Jack said that wasn't any of his concern.

Again I asked if he would loan me the $400, Jack said "You do not have a job, and is far as I know, you are in deep financial trouble." Again I tried to explain how I got in the financial trouble, but was cut off again by Jack saying it wasn't his problem. I knew I was wasting my time, so I bid him good day and thanked him for his time.

As fate would have it, as I exited the winery that I helped build , I noticed Craig and Les who were working for Jack that day, were leaving in Les's truck. As I watch them turn out of the drive toward Muscatine, I wondered if they knew I was going to be right behind them.

I followed them into the Blains Farm & Fleet parking lot, as Craig got out of the passenger side, as I pulled up. I told him sorry about your luck, and that you better be looking for a place to live. He replied by telling me that there was a warrant for my arrest, for stealing the white truck. I just chuckled, and told them they should've paid. Craig replied; "Then sue him for the $500!", then turned and walked away. I just could not let him have the last word, so I told him. "It's tens of thousands now.", and drove away.

CHAPTER 5

Hurricane Diane

Diane called the police at 11:16 AM on June 3rd to report the truck stolen. In the report, her statement is; she purchased the truck from me on June 1st for $100 and then on June 2nd I came and borrowed the truck, saying that I was going to bring it right back. She said, "I then went to the county treasurer and reported the title stolen before she had a chance to transfer it".

***

Please see; Davenport Police report # 05-11668.

***

When Diane presented the title that was signed, and dated March 28, 2005. The clerk confiscated the title, and bill of sale, and told her it's a civil matter. Diane dare not go before any Judge, because she was in breech of contract. So she had to forge a new bill of sale, and make up a story for the police.

Forging the new bill of sale was easy, because she had plenty of examples of my signature to copy. Her only problem was that she did not have a title. If Detective Denger would have made just one phone call to the Scott County Treasurers office, and retrieved the title, he would have discovered it was signed on March 28, 2005, not June 1, 2005. He also would have discovered a bill of sale dated March 28, 2005, this which would have proved, that their version is a forgery.

***

Monday June 6th; armed with a cure or quit notice I drove to my home, when I arrived Colin opened the door, and greeted me guardedly. I noticed a strange male sitting at the table I said to him "You must be Diane's father?" He replied that he was her uncle, so I asked him what Diane's legal last name was.

He replied, "That was none of my business and that I was to get out of her house this instant!" I informed him that I owned this property and that the only person that had legal right to live there was Colin. Once again he told me to leave my property. I was thinking so this was how they were going to play it. So I left, and went to the closest pay phone and called the police, then returned to Wapello Avenue and waited.

Why Chris Brandle conspired with his Niece Diane, to file a false police report will be a mystery, but it is a fact. That on June 6, 2005 at 11:30, Police report # 05-11942 was filed. In this report, he accuses me of threats and intimidation of 22 year Colin Shellabarger. Colin has never filed a report with the police, even though he was being interviewed by a Corporal of the Davenport Police Department only minutes after the alleged assault occurred.

There is also the discrepancy between his statement, and the statement that Diane made in Report # 05-12191. In his statement, 05-11942, he also said I used profanity in the presence of minors. Not that I had physically assaulted Kristine, and threaten to rape & kill her, as Diane claims.

I must apologize however, for I did reply to the question from Kristine, "What are you going to do?" By answering, "Sue the s#!t out of them." Beyond that, I conducted myself with dignity and decorum, considering the circumstances.

**

First to arrive was Corporal Todd, and as I was answering his questions, a detective whose name I did not catch arrived. They exchanged briefings; then Cpl. Todd, and I proceeded to serve the cure or quit notice. Cpl. Todd was kind enough to inform Colin that this did not concern him, and explained that when Craig and Diane left, they were not to take anything that did not belong to them. Colin replied that; Craig and Diane said they had paid. Cpl. Todd informed him that was up to a court of law. Colin confirmed that he understood, and that he would give them the notice. I told Colin I was sorry, and that I did not know what was going to happen.

It was around 8:30 PM when Craig called my Brother Michael's house. Michael handed me the phone and said it's Craig. Craig's statement to me was, "What I was trying to accomplish?" I replied; that you and Diane are in default of our agreement and are now liable for all my expenses, and that you are to vacate my home immediately.

He once again told me that there was a warrant for my arrest, and the quit or cure notice wasn't worth the paper it was printed on. I told him to get out of my house and hung up the phone. Michael asked me what I thought was going to happen. I replied; "I don't know?"

CHAPTER 6

Eye of the Storm

Wednesday June 9th; another road trip from Muscatine, to the Scott County Courthouse. It cost $50 at the clerk of court to file for an Action for Forcible Entry, and Detainer. The Sheriff's office civil division charged me $30 to serve notice to appear, this should occur at around 4:30 PM.

My troubles are only just beginning. As it stands right now, I have the bank taken care of, I owe MasterCard two months payment, I owe the mortgage company two months payment, have no idea how much the phone bill is, I have no idea how much the water bill is, or how much I owe the city of Davenport for recycling and garbage pickup.

I have gone to the storage unit where the Corvette, and other things I moved out of the house are, and have gotten clothes, the computer, and accessories. I have also changed the lock.

I have put in applications at the temporary employment agencies places in Muscatine, and have started making phone calls looking for a job. Thankfully Mike & Lisa are letting me stay at their home.

9:37 AM June 9, 2005; the police arrive at 3927 Wapello Avenue to meet with a visibly shaken Diane Merks. She tells the police an elaborate story on how, I give her my house and left the country in search of a wife, and now I've been stalking & threatening her since I returned from Vietnam.

***

Please see; Davenport police report # 05-12191.

***

Friday June 10th; I have been informed by Scott County Sheriff's office; that the hearing will be at 1 PM June 14. I am glad that this upcoming weekend will be filled with activities such as Lisa's nephew, Troy's wedding. It will be occurring Saturday afternoon. I will be spending most of the day with my nephew Matthew, who needs constant attention. I will also be working on immigration form I-130, so that I can get that filed.

***

Saturday June 11th; Diane calls the police around midnight to report an attempted burglary. I was a sleep in Muscatine IA, twenty-five miles away.

***

Please see; Davenport police report # 50-12417.

***

Monday June 14th; to say that I wasn't anxious about the upcoming hearing would be a lie. My brother Michael and I arrived at the courthouse around 12:45 PM. I checked in, and we proceeded to wait for my turn at justice.

Michael was the first to see Craig at the sheriff's desk. He commented; "I wonder what that is about". We would find out in 20 minutes, when the Sergeant Bailiff approached me and asked if he could talk to me outside.

We were met by a detective from the sheriff's department, he asked me about what I was doing at the courthouse today. I gave him the file, and explained the situation. He asked me if I had a gun. I replied no I don't carry one. He then asked if he could search me, I agreed.

When he was finished, he commented that I didn't have a gun, and why was my ex-wife outside telling everyone that I had a gun, and was going to kill everybody in the courthouse.

I replied that I did not have an ex-wife, and I did not have any idea what was going on outside. He thanked me for my time, and said that I could return to the courtroom, Michael and I returned to the courtroom to wait.

The case was called, I approached the bench, and the judge called the case again, and asked me if they were here? I replied; "They were here earlier". He called the case again. He reviewed the folder, and asked me if I wanted the property immediately. I indicated that I did. He entered the order, and then directed me to the clerk who was at that time having problems with the copier.

After about 10 minutes of fighting with the copier, she gathered up the orders to take to a different copier. During this time Diane, Craig, and

Colin had entered the courtroom, I did not see them enter because my back was to the door, and I was at the front of the courtroom.

As the clerk left, I followed her to where my brother was seated, and waited for her return. It took about 20 minutes for her to return with four different people's orders, which she passed out. I took the defendant copies, and handed them to Craig. Then said; "Courts over and you lost." Diane whined that she did not get to tell her story, I just turned and left.

Outside Michael and I were talking, and it was decided to go directly to my house. When we arrived we were stunned into silence, everything was gone, and I mean everything from the bird feeders to the shelves in the garage.

CHAPTER 7

The Rest of the Storm

It is estimated to be $125,000 worth of property that my friend of 18 years was supposed to protect, and they stole it all. Michael asked me what I was going to do. I replied; "The first thing is to call the police.", which I did. I then called the insurance company to report the theft.

I used up about 45 minutes on Michael's cell phone, talking to the insurance company. When I was finished, Michael pointed out that the police still weren't here, so I called 911 again. As I was talking to the operator, a squad car drove by, I told the operator that the officers were here and then hung up.

The officer's asked my brother and I for identification, after they had confirmed who we were, they proceeded to take my statement. It took about 25 minutes to relay all the important information. During this time a second patrol unit arrived, this officer proceeded to talk to one of the original officers.

***

At this time I was informed that I was under arrest, my brother was the one to ask what for? The officers replied; burglary, theft, forgery, stalking, and harassment, the bond had been set at $35,000. I was handcuffed, and then escorted to the back of a police car. This was something that I was not expecting when the day began.

The destination surprised me, instead of going to the police department to talk to the detectives handling the case; I was taken directly to the county jail. As the jailers started to process me in, I became greatly concerned that no one had bothered to ask me any questions about any of the allegations.

The hardest part of the processing was when pretrial release was interviewing me, and I was trying to explain that yes I am married, and no we are not separated, and that I did not want to leave her to come back to America. The jailer behind the main-desk was interfering with the interview by yelling at me to just answer the questions. They were acting like I raped a child, and were not grasping the concept, that I had only landed in the country 14 days ago. And that I was totally innocent, and was actually the victim.

With that extremely painful ordeal behind me I was shown to a holding cell with two steel beds, and four other people. As we settled into the conversation what are you here for; I found it deeply disturbing that everyone else was also innocent; it was going to be a very long night.

※※※

Video court the next morning was to see things get even stranger. The judge who the day before gave me an order to throw Diane out on the street, was now issuing an order of protection and increasing my bond by $10,000 because I was a threat to society. The only motion I was granted, was for a bond reduction hearing the next morning, and a court appointed attorney.

My only hope was that the court-appointed attorney John Molyneaux would get to see me today, so he would know what was going on. Then tomorrow he could convince the Judge that everything was mistake, and the bond would be reduced to 10% to the clerk. I was taken back to the holding cell, and told that very soon I would be moved to general population.

The attorney from the public defender's office arrived up in the afternoon. As the conversation moved from pleasantries to business, I began growing concerned. The one person in the system who was to be my advocate sat across from me, telling me I had done some serious things. As I once again tried to explain the whole situation to him, he kept asking me if my name is Kenneth Fry and to stick to preliminaries. I finally told him to call my brother Michael, and he would explain everything.

I would come to find out, that when he spoke to Lisa, he asked if I had psychological problems or I was on drugs, because I kept rambling on about being in Vietnam. He told Lisa that I was not old enough to be in Vietnam, and an insanity defense would not work. I wish that I could have a recording of the conversation, because I did not hear it. But to this day John Molyneaux still has not grasped the fact that I was innocent, and actually the victim.

※※※

Wednesday June 16th; video court day two, different Judge worst attitude. As the county attorney, and pretrial release people slander me on the record. My advocate from the public defenders office just sits there agreeing with the state. Once again, the Judge on record said; "You have done some scary stuff, and that she would be scared too. So for the safety of society, my bond will remain the same and there will be no 10 percent to the court!" Once again, no one grasped that I was actually the victim.

As I was escorted back to the cell, my mind was racing a million miles an hour, I had no idea what was I going to do. The first person that came to see me after the hearing was my advocate from the public defender's office. Our conversation consisted of me asking him if he knew what he was doing, and his reply; "I am going on vacation for two weeks, and I do not accept phone calls, write a letter".

My second visitor was Michael; our conversation consisted of me telling him that my attorney was an idiot, and that if I didn't get out of here they were going to railroad me with 35 years. I also told him that I didn't know how I would pay him back if he made my bail. Yet he took $5000 out of their savings account to pay the bail bonds company.

***

Thank you again Mike & Lisa!

CHAPTER 8

The Aftermath

I did however make a huge mistake the day Michael got me out of jail; I should have gone straight to the Davenport Police Department and filed a report with internal affairs. Then maybe I would have had been able to sue the city, but I wanted the police to prosecute Diane for theft, obstruction of justice, conspiracy, and false statements to the police, so I did not want to make them angry.

My next bit of luck was, Michael's mother Linda informed me, that where she worked they needed a maintenance person. I told her that I needed at least $12 an hour, and what did they produce. The next day she told me that they wanted to talk, I stopped by Temp associate's employment agency to let them know that Plasticraft wanted to interview me. The interview went well except for the fact, that I was extremely overqualified for the position. We made final arrangements on a start date, and on salary.

※※※

Now that I have the income problem solved, I have two more problems. The first is finding competent legal representation, second is to start the claims process with the insurance company. Finding competent legal representation turned out to be extremely difficult, because not having the $5000 for the retainer was the stopping point of the conversation.

I finally found help with retired judge James Weaver. After a lengthy interview, and verifying the facts, he helped by only charging me for actual hours worked after he completed them. The first thing he advised me on was to let the public defender handle the arraignment, so we could get the trial information without Jim going to Davenport. I was to meet with the public defender, and get the trial information from him.

Insurance Special Investigator William Fisher has been trying to get in contact with me since the 15th; we finally made contact on Thursday the 17th. We have a lengthy phone conversation, and made arrangements to meet in Davenport so that he can record my statement, and take pictures of the property.

Unfortunately after many interviews, and months of investigation, the insurance company has determined that all of my property that was stolen. Is not covered by my insurance policy, because the police are not treating it as a crime, and without the assistance of the States Attorney, it is being treated as a civil matter.

Detective Denger told Special Investigator William Fisher; that as far as the Davenport Police Department, and the State's Attorneys office are concerned. Kenneth Fry is the perpetrator of violent felonies, and Diane Merks is the victim of those crimes, and all the property is hers.

CHAPTER 9

Total Incompetence

July 2005; the day of the arraignment has arrived. My public defender has returned from vacation, and is in the best of moods. As he greets me, he informs me that the county attorney has dropped the charges, my heart races. We go into an empty courtroom, and he proceeds to tell me about this great deal he has got for me.

The county attorney has reduced the charges to 2 simple misdemeanors. Count one; misuse of official documents. Count two; harassment. I was stunned, I requested the file, and then proceeded to take it away from him.

What I saw inside chilled me to the core. The only thing there was the original indictment, and my NCIC federal background check. I told my public defender that he was fired, and then I proceeded into the next courtroom where the arraignments were being held.

As I enter the courtroom he pushes past me, and goes through the gate, then proceeds to address the court. His monologue consists of Mr. Fry has rejected the generous offer from the state and insists upon a trial.

For the record I proceeded to fire the public defender again and address the clerk. I requested that trial information be produced per the code of Iowa.

Once again, the public defender tried to address the court in my behalf. By saying; that the state had made a generous offer, therefore didn't compile information. I must confess that I lost my temper, and told the public defender; "what part of your fired didn't you get, now shut up and sit down!"

The clerk directed the bailiff to get the file from me. I surrendered the file, and asked when the judge was going to be here. Just then the county attorney entered the courtroom, and the clerk informs him that I have requested a trial, and need the trial information. He acknowledges this, and exits the same door he just entered.

✳✳✳

I asked the clerk when the judge was going to be here; she replied in about 45 minutes, and then asked me what I was going to do without an attorney. I informed her that I had retained James Weaver, and that he directed me to return with that file. She told me that I could not have custody of it, and to take this note, which the bailiff handed to me, to Jim.

She looked at the calendar, and told me the arraignment would be rescheduled for next week. I thanked her, and turned to exit the courtroom. The fired public defender wished me good luck; I replied that he would've sent me to prison.

I return to Muscatine, and report to Jim what had occurred during court. He told me not to worry about it, everything would be ok. To confess; I am having a hard time believing that. The next court date has been scheduled, now the only thing to do is, work, eat, and sleep.

PART 2

CHAPTER 1

The Injustice Begins

The day has arrived for the state to produce trial information, during the 30 minute drive from Muscatine to Davenport, Jim and I reviewed what will be taking place today. Basically we will be entering a not guilty plea, and the state's attorney will be producing all of the information that will be used against me at trial.

When we arrive Jim directs me to have a seat, and proceeds through a side door. He returns 15 minutes later with the file, and hands it to me, then tells me not to get upset. As I read through the trial information I start to chuckle.

Jim looks at me like I have lost my mind; I smile and continue to read through the various police reports. When I finish; I tell Jim that he shouldn't have to put more than a couple hours to get the charges dismissed. With our business finished for the day, we depart for Muscatine.

***

August 2005; I have been working large amounts of overtime trying to fix the financial catastrophe that has occurred, Diane Merks has been subpoenaed to appear in depositions, and has called the police to report that I have violated the restraining order by trying to force my way in their new rental property at 3709 South Concorde Street; Davenport, Iowa. At 1:30 in the afternoon, Thursday August 4th. I was 30 miles away at work.

***

Please see; Davenport police report # 05-17408

***

August 16th; the day of depositions has arrived. Jim and I have prepared a list of questions for Ms. Merks to answer. When Jim and I arrive at the county attorney's office, we are directed to a room where a stenographer waited. The county attorney said something to Jim that I did not hear, and they left. I made small talk with the stenographer, when I noticed two men in suits standing outside the room having a conversation of what the subject appeared to be was me.

When they noticed, that I had noticed them, they moved off. Shortly after that my attorney returned, and asked me what my work hours had been. I replied; "1 PM to 11 PM". He then asked me what the phone number was, I did not know it off the top of my head, but told him the name and location.

As I, and the stenographer conversed about what that was about. Special Investigator William Fisher came into the room. He speaks to the stenographer, telling her that she probably wasn't going to be needed. He then tells me that he's going to interview Diane Merks, and that he really couldn't give me any more information, but my attorney should be here shortly.

Jim was ecstatic when he returned. He explained that they had issued another arrest warrant for me, and that they were going to arrest me when depositions were over. However, in light of the facts that I was at work when I was accused of trying to break into Diane's rental property on Concorde Avenue at 1:30 PM on August 4th, and Diane Merks was refusing to be deposed, all of the charges had been dismissed.

The county attorney entered the room, and proceeded to tell me that all of the charges were dismissed, and all the cost would be bore by the state. I should note however; that attorney fees would not be covered by this statement, and the public defender that I had fired, submitted an invoice to the court for services rendered which they paid without question. Now I owe the clerk of court $135, and cannot renew my license plates or conduct other business until this is paid.

CHAPTER 2

Legal Limbo

As Jim and I drove toward Muscatine we talked of the civil action against Diane Merks for slander, defamation of character, and breach of contract. Jim said that we could probably get a judgment for $150,000. I was curious how a judgment could be enforced.

Now this August day I no longer have to worry about going to prison, but I am on the other side of the Earth from my wife, and we are as poor as church mice.

***

September 2005; I am still working in Wilton, I have cleaned and moved back into our home, I also have half of the yard cleaned up, and let me tell you it was no easy task, the weeds have had since the middle of June to thrive. In the middle of the mess I found a departing gift from Craig, a pile of broken asbestos house siding. Every time I have seen it removed, it was a HAZ- MAT situation.

Life goes on; I've been trying to get back to a semblance of normalcy, so I thought deer hunting this fall would be good for me. That meant I needed to speak with Jack, I did not know what kind of reception I would receive.

Jack took a while to answer the door; he was preparing to shower for an evening out. He greeted me cordially enough; however I felt an undertone of wariness that had not existed between us before.

I asked how life was treating him; he replied that he couldn't complain. I got right to point, and asked if I could go deer hunting this year. Jack inquired about my legal problems, I explained that all had been dismissed and hopefully the Police Department and county attorney were now recognizing me as the victim.

He seemed quite surprised at this, saying that Craig and Diane had been telling him I was in prison for 35 years. I assured him that all was well with my legal situation; however we were financially destroyed by

Craig and Diane's misconduct. Jack said he didn't want to get involved in the situation. However he invited me in to their home, and offered me a cold drink.

We sat, and discussed the fact that Jack had promised Carl, an old friend of his, the right to hunt the vineyard this year. I told Jack I understood, because I was supposed to be in Viet Nam.

As we made small talk, I came to realize that we had no future as the friends he thought we were, because we believe in completely different things, like what the definition of friend is.

CHAPTER 3

Not the Victim

October 2005; I have been told by Special Investigator Fisher that the DPD still consider me a perpetrator of felonies against a minor, and refuse to help with my complaint. So I make a trip to the Police station, and asked the desk officer at the Davenport Police Department if I could speak to someone from internal affairs.

She asked if she could have more information, in case it did not have to be referred to internal affairs. I complied and told her the story. After listening attentively, she said that the Lieutenant in charge of the criminal investigations division was who I needed to see.

I did not have to wait long for the lieutenant, and he escorted me right to his office. He asked how they can help me, and I turned over to him the police reports that I received as trial information. I sat quietly as he read through the many pages, when he was done he asked me to clarify some things.

The conversation from that point lasted 45 minutes, when we were done he assured me that a proper investigation would occur. I thanked him for his time and departed the police station. Once again, I got my hopes up that I would finally receive justice.

***

I checked with the Police Department a few weeks later, and was interviewed by the sergeant from the theft squad. He sat in disbelief, as I try to explain the complex situation that has occurred. He seemed to have trouble with the fact that no one contacted me, or made any attempt to verify the facts. He also told me that the nature of this case moved it out of his jurisdiction, and into the criminal investigation division, and the reason he was here was because Sergeant Glandon was on vacation, and they needed more information from me. I was told that the next time I came in that I would speak to Sgt. Glandon.

November 2005; I spoke with Sgt. Glandon. I received quite a different reception than I had the previous two times. This time I was treated as the perpetrator of crimes against women and minors.

Needless to say our conversation was not very polite, nor was it very quiet. Our interview ended with Sgt. Glandon telling me, that if he had his way he would lock me up. I bid him a good day, and departed the Police Station.

Hopes dashed again that the Government would see the mistake they had made, and fix it.

***

Thanksgiving at Mike & Lisa's is a wondrous event, just picture if you will the most perfect holiday scene. Enough food for 50 people, Lisa does an excellent job every year. I did however; miss my wife terribly, so I occupied my time by entertaining my nephew Mathew Robert, who is severely disabled. He really enjoys hearing Harleys on Hot Rods Driving by.

December 2005; I finally interview with the detective that is handling my case. Detective Martin greets me warmly, and proceeds with the interview professionally. The interview is thorough, and very detailed. However at the end of it, Detective Martin informs me that it would be up to the county attorney to file obstruction, and false statement charges, against Craig and Diane. He did assure me, that he would do everything he could to bring charges for the theft of all the property. I thanked him for his time, and departed.

The end of the old year, and the beginning of the new bring many parties and festivities. Considering I spent Thanksgiving with Mike and Lisa, it was decided that I would drive my Mother to my Brother Douglas's house for Christmas Eve. Then spend Christmas Day at my Sister Tina's House. All in all I had a very good time considering I turned 43 this year, and I miss Lan terribly.

CHAPTER 4

Something Good, a Whole lot Bad

January 15, 2006; I receive some great news in the mail today. The letter from the Department of Homeland Security stated; the petition had been approved, and was being forwarded to the national visa processing center. The last I knew, it was going to be three years before she would receive her visa. I don't know if this is good or if this is bad. I would dearly love to have my wife with me, but when it comes to doing paperwork for the federal government I think we are in big trouble, because our finances have been wiped out, and I am barely making enough to cover the bills.

Everyone is thrilled with the unexpected news, and question me relentlessly about what is going to happen. I can only reply; that I don't have a clue.

January 19, 2006; I receive a glowing pre-employment evaluation, the maintenance manager completes the 10 page form the company requires. Then he faxes all of the information to the headquarters in Albertville, AL for their final approval.

February 2, 2006; I make my first round, and find Chris my supervisor working on a press. He says; you're in the right place, and then asks me to tell him why he should let me continue working here.

To say I was a little lost would be an understatement; I had no idea what he was talking about, so I asked him. He replied; "He didn't know if it was incompetence or negligence, but wanted to know why I didn't look at the mould that had gotten steel in it. And that he had fixed it this morning, by using a brass rod and pushed the steel back into the manifold!".

I asked; "How is that maintenance problem, when production personnel used contaminated regrind for the tenth time?" Chris stated; "I have already told the plant manager that you are gone'" I said to him, and then I should punch out, he replied "yep". I wished him good luck, and proceeded to the time clock.

❃❃❃

To say that the staff at Temp associates was a little confused as to why I would be fired after seven months; would be an understatement. I went on to explain, I was to sign a W-4 to become a full-time employee today. After a lengthy post-employment interview, I was told that they would do everything they could to find me a new position somewhere else.

I did the only thing I could; I went and filed for unemployment insurance. Of course Temp associates denied the claim. After a week of getting their story straight, Plasticraft finally called Temp associates with their version of what happened.

The day of the hearing with the Administrative Law Judge for Iowa workforce development was quite the shock for me. During this hearing Temp associates statement was; I had walked out during a disciplinary reprimand. My pleas of, none of that is in writing, and it isn't even close to the truth fell upon deaf ears. My claim was denied, based on it was a voluntary quit without cause.

I immediately filed an appeal, it was set for 30 days later, which give me time to try and salvage the situation. The only solution I could come up with was to get a statement from one of the people who were witness to the incident.

***

Mid-February, my repeated calls to the Scout County attorney's office to find out why Craig and Diane have not been arrested, have finally bore fruit. I have a meeting with Bill Davis elected official. The first meeting only lasted about 15 minutes, but it looked very promising. I told Mr. Davis entire story, and had answered his numerous questions. At this point he was kind enough to say he had some investigating to do, and he would get back to me.

When he did get back to me to schedule an interview, it was three days later. This meeting was to change my whole outlook toward the government. Mr. Davis told me he had prosecutorial discretion, and he would not pursue charges of any kind, against anyone in the situation, because it was a civil matter.

When I questioned him about Diane, and Kristine lying to the police, he said that he couldn't prove that they lied, and this matter was closed as far as he was concerned.

***

So that is the way it is in America now. If you are ex-law enforcement, you can lie to the police, have someone prosecuted, steal everything they own, and it's a civil matter.

As I leave the county courthouse, I'm thinking, if it's a civil matter then I should go file a federal lawsuit for false arrest and malicious prosecution. It is also time to do some interviewing of attorneys who will be willing to work with me with little upfront expenditures.

CHAPTER 5

Judge Judy

My next move is to file small claims against Diane Merks, and her daughter Kristine for false statements to the police, and false arrest. I filed four claims. Two against Diane, and two against Kristine; the filing fees total $200.

***

What a surprise this day has been, a special delivery from the producers of Judge Judy. They want to know if I would be interested in appearing on the television show. I immediately call California, at which point I realize it is only 8:00 in the morning on the West Coast, I leave a message.

May Johnson, a producer from the show returns my call that afternoon, we have a lengthy discussion about the situation, and do I think it is something I would do? I replied; that I would not have a problem with it, but I had serious doubts if Diane would even consider going on TV. I was going on the assumption that she wouldn't answer the complaint let alone appear before a Judge. May replied; let me handle that, I'm pretty sure that I can get Diane to agree.

At that point I had nothing to lose and everything to gain, so I agreed. Numerous phone calls and faxes later, all of the arrangements had been made for our appearance to be recorded on the Judge Judy show March 29.

***

In my wildest dreams, do I dream that Craig will actually go on TV.

CHAPTER 6

No Civil Rights

Every attorney that I've contacted, has basically told me that I don't have a case. I find this hard to believe, so I go to the clerk's office for the Southern district of Iowa, and request the paperwork for filing Pro Se. I complete the paperwork, and attach all necessary documents. Then pay the $250 filing fee, before it goes up on Monday to over $300. The clerk instructs me on how to work with the waiver of service, so that I do not have to pay to have the complaint served on the defendant's.

My first stop was at the Scott County administration office. There I was met by a bureaucrat, who told me that it was not a real lawsuit so they did not have to comply with the waiver of service. I question her if she had actually read the paperwork that she was supposed to read. The reply was that it was not a real lawsuit and they didn't have to do anything.

I returned to the clerk's office and explained what had transpired; he prepared all the official filings for service. I took the paperwork to the Scott County sheriff's office civil division, and paid to have the complaint served on the defendants.

Now the cost is over $300 in filing fees just to get heard in the federal court system, I believe there is a coordinated effort to eliminate the number of lawsuits against the government for wrongful acts.

Not even a week has passed and I've received letters from the judge and the clerks of the Southern District of Iowa, telling me that the case has been dismissed, because there is no constitutional protection against false arrest and malicious prosecution.

Now I understand why things happened the way they did, every official involved knew that they were immune from any repercussions, no matter what their actions, they just did not care whose lives they destroyed.

I feel that the $300 I spent was well worth the letter saying that a citizen unlawfully prosecuted has no protections or recourse against the people who swore to uphold and defend the Constitution.

CHAPTER 7

Hollywood

March 28, 2006; the Hyatt on Sunset Boulevard is a very nice place, and tomorrow we tape Judge Judy. As with every day, I am up before the birds with a lot on my mind. First-order business is to find a small café that won't charge me eight dollars for coffee. What luck, around the corner is a Starbucks. Now armed with muffin and coffee, I prepare for a whole new experience of being on TV.

As directed, I call for a cab at the appropriate time so I will arrive at the studio at 8 AM. Now I know what a green room is like, if I could have slept a few more hours I could have saved what I spent on breakfast, there was a rather impressive buffet. But come to think of it, at that point I was probably way too nervous to eat, so it was a good thing that I went on my morning excursion.

The wait was occupied by doing paperwork, and reviewing the sequence of events that would occur during taping. Randy Caspersen, the Production Assistant told me that Craig had made the trip to California and was going to appear.

I spent a total of 35 minutes waiting until there was a cancellation and I was next, so off to make up I went. At first I was kind of anxious, but as I told what had happened, I forgot all about the cameras. I must say that the whole thing was rather fast, I do not believe we spent more than 20 to 25 minutes taping.

When we got to the part where Judge Judy is asking me about the police report she is reading, the one where Diane is telling the Davenport Police, that I have been convicted of attempted murder. Judge Judy asked me if that was true. I responded that that was not true; she then asked if I had been imprisoned before.

I replied yes; she asked me what for. I replied that is confidential, and here is my confidential NCIC, offering her the document. After reading it, Judge Judy directed Bert to return it to me, and proceeded to ask Diane and Craig some very hard questions.

I guess she did not like their answers, because she turned and asked me how long I spent in jail. When I replied three days, she awarded me the full $5000. At the end of it I went out first, but Bert the bailiff called me back and let Diane go first. Instead of waiting right by the door and listening to what she had to say, I waited up by the bench and looked at all the people who had just watched Craig and Diane humiliate them selves on national television.

I then witnessed someone from the audience being told to leave; a floor coordinator approached a young woman who was sitting behind me. She approached the audience member and said, "You were chewing gum and talking during the whole taping, so you have to leave!"

When it was my turn to be interviewed, I was so stunned that something actually had gone right I was speechless. I believe I was asked about the allegations Diane had made against me in her post show interview. I responded "not true". I was also asked about Judge Judy's ruling I replied, " Justice is served" then I had to sign some more forms, after that I was escorted back out the same door I came in.

***

There was a surreal feeling as I stood outside the studio waiting for the cab to take me back to the hotel, it seemed like I was standing out there for half an hour, but in actuality it was only 10 minutes. If you care to view the episode, the show is on YOUTUBE under Nervous Kojak betrayed by brainless rednecks, or just GOOGLE search Kenneth Ralph Fry, and remember to watch parts 1&2 please.

Back at the hotel I changed into T-shirt, shorts, and running shoes, and headed out for lunch. As I was exiting the lobby of the Hyatt on Sunset who do I see but ZZ Top getting into a pink convertible Cadillac.

I spend most of the day making a big loop out of Sunset Boulevard. Down the street from the hotel I discovered the Ranch House restaurant, I will return later that evening after my walk, shower, and a nap. Until then I have a tender roast combo at KFC for lunch midway through my walk through the Hollywood Hills. The rest of my walk, returned me to the hotel for my much need nap.

My nap is disturbed by the paparazzi in the parking lot below my window, taking photos. There are two other musical groups at the hotel, Enuffs Enuff and BOW WOW. I watch the commotion for about 10 minutes and decide to make some phone calls. Everyone is excited to hear about the outcome, and is shocked by the fact that Craig showed up to be taped.

Talking on the phone until suppertime, I went for short walk to the Ranch House restaurant. I started a most wonderful dinning experience with a perfect Black Russian, made with two parts Stoli & one part Kahlua; no ice. I decided upon a cowboy cut of prime rib, and a full-bodied dark beer on tap, of which I had two.

When my meal arrived I was in awe, the platter was as long as a keyboard and held a 14 oz. steak, a pound of garlic mashed potatoes, and a pound of broccoli and corn mix. It was all I had to eat most of the steak, while trying not to waste the rest of the meal. I spent under $50, and kind of wished there wasn't so much food because I could not eat it all.

CHAPTER 8

Accomplices Revealed

April 2006; I decided to take a chance and talk to Jack. I was greeted cordially enough, and Jack was surprised to hear about the trip to California, and the Judge Judy taping. This surprised me, because I thought that Craig would have told jack everything, and I said as much to Jack.

His reply was that Craig was no longer a trusted friend, and not allowed on the property. This statement made me very curious, so I asked what had happened. The story that Jack told, made me see red. He explained that in December, Craig needed a place to move all of his property, because they were being evicted from their rental property.

Jack allowed Craig to store all of my stolen property, at the vacant photo lab in Bluegrass, IA. However it was only to be short term, because the property was being sold. The problems started when it was time to close on the property, and Craig still had not moved anything, so the deal did not happen. This cost Jack a lot of money, and aggravation.

At this point I reminded Jack that most everything that was stored; was the property that Craig stole from me. The look on Jack's face was one of pure terror, as he realized that he just confessed that he was involved in the theft of over $150,000 in property; to the victim of said crime.

Needless to say, at this point Jack stated that he was very busy and asked me to leave. I have no idea what he did after I left, but I would bet that he called an Attorney.

CHAPTER 9

It keeps Getting Worst

On the career front, still no job, but I have had several interviews with promises of second interviews. I think I will have a very hard time finding a job in Iowa.

In hopes of getting some publicity, and maybe some help. I have designed two flyers for when Judge Judy airs; I have also contacted WQAD in Moline and have informed them of the situation.

I am planning to have quite the media event; hopefully I will have the book done so that I can use the publicity to help sell books. I have contacted several self publishing companies to get information on self publishing this book.

***

Mid- April 2006 more bad news from the Scott County judicial system, Diane somehow convinces the clerk of court in Scott County, that Judge Judy heard the two outstanding civil actions against her daughter Kristine Garcia. Which is the farthest thing from the truth, Judge Judy refused to hear anything from Kristine.

On Saturday I received an order from the clerk's office dismissing all pending cases because they were submitted to a foreign jurisdiction. The first thing I think is, nice of them to mail this thing so that I get it on a Saturday so there's nothing I can do about it.

Monday morning I went to the clerk's office, presented the order and asked about it. I received nothing but hostility and apathy, from the staff. Finally the judge made his appearance, he did not have a clue what was going on. After not wanting to hear what I had to say, he made another ruling telling me that it was still dismissed, but if I wanted to file an appeal it would be $500 apiece.

I asked him what his name was; he said it was on the bottom. I replied; I could not read that illegible scrawl and would he please spell his name for me. He replied Gene Dwyer; I thanked him for his time, and left the courthouse.

After a long internet search, I found the web site for the state judicial oversight committee, and filled out a complaint. Those nice people sent me an appeal form, and basically told me to take a flying leap. So instead of Kristine going in front of a judge and explaining why she told police that I tried to force my way into her home when I was really 30 miles away at work. Nothing is going to happen.

✻✻✻

May 24th 2006 9:44 a.m.; all dressed for job hunting. I pick up the remote to shut the TV off, I see Diane on the TV, and I run to the neighbors. Thankfully they're there. We watched the last part of the show as Judge Judy hands down her decision, everyone busted out laughing when Craig raised his hand and Judge Judy told him to put it down.

After the show, it starts to dawn on me that now I am really screwed because, I was not prepared for the show to air so soon, so I missed out on all of the publicity that would have helped resolve some of the financial issues.

Now I have no legal standing, with no legal recourse, and to make things even worst, I have no job, no prospects of a job, and my wife is on the other side of the world.

✻✻✻

THE END

✻✻✻

POST SCRIPT

The biggest mistake I made during this whole situation was to co-operate with pre-trial release. If I would have told them to take a flying leap, the assistant county attorney would have had to stand in front of the Judge, and say that I have no criminal record, because it takes 3 to 4 days to get sealed records from the IDCI data bank. I should have gotten out for 10% to the court.

***

Forever Grateful

If it were not for all of the help, everyone at the Temple of the Flowing Waters gave me during this nightmare, I do not know what would have happened. I am eternally in your debt. Thank you, very much!!!!

Please send a donation to;

Temple of the Flowing Waters
2834 River Road
Muscatine, IA 52761

Thank you very much!

***

REFERENCE

Davenport Police Report....................#0511668
Davenport Police Report....................#0511942
Davenport Police Report.............#0512191 Page 1
Davenport Police Report.............#0512191 Page 2
Davenport Police Report.............#0512417 Page 1
Davenport Police Report.............#0512417 Page 2
Scott County Complaint & Affidavit.... #FECR279164
Davenport Police Report.............#0517408 Page 1
Davenport Police Report.............#0517408 Page 2
www.iowacourts.state.ia.us ....Case Dismissed

***

KENNETH RALPH FRY

DAVENPORT POLICE DEPARTMENT
INCIDENT REPORT

0511668

at	Area	Force					Prepared by		Serial Nbr	Initial
2	2B	N	06-14-05	15:19	0667		GLOVER		0562	

VEHICLE THEFT	Business	Location 3927 WAPELLO AV

| me of ccurrence | MO DA YR 06 02 05 | Time 07:30 | to | MO DA YR 06 02 05 | Time 07:30 | Day of Week THURSDAY | Time of Report | MO DA YR 06 03 05 | Time 11:16 |

ode	Last, First M	S/R	Home Address	DOB	Home Phone
M	MERKS, DIANE MARIE	F W	3927 WAPELLO AV DAVENPORT	01-10-69	563-940-2180
S	FRY, KENNETH RALPH	M W		01-02-63	

```
         Officer#    Date       Time
           0562    06-03-05   12:01
```

Media Information

On Friday, 03 June '05 at about 1116 hours, the complainant called the station to report the theft of her recently purchased vehicle by the seller.

Supplement Information

On Friday, 03 June '05 at about 1116 hours the complainant called the station to report the theft of her newly purchased vehicle.

Interview with Ms. Diane Marie Merks

Ms. Merks stated that on 01 June '05, she purchased a White, 1988 Chevy 4 x 4 pickup truck, from Kenneth Fry. She paid $100.00 cash for the truck and received the signed title and a bill of sale.

Yesterday, at about 0730 hours, Mr. Fry came to her residence and asked her if he could borrow the truck for the day. She stated that he could but he had to have the truck back by 1700 hours. He became very upset and began striking the truck with his fist. He was then told that he could not take the truck at all. He then stated that he was taking the truck anyway and that he was not bringing it back. He also told her that he was going to report his title stolen.

Ms. Merks went to get the new title for the truck. She was advised that Mr. Fry had already been there and stated that the title had been stolen. She attempted to persuade them that the vehicle had been purchased by her and provided the signed title as well as the signed bill of sale.
End of Interview

Ms. Merks stated that the reason she did not report the theft yesterday was because Mr. Fry is a long time friend of her fiance. She thought she would give Mr. Fry the benefit of the doubt due to his connection with her fiance.

Unit #107
R.F.Glover #562

RECORDS/SUPERVISOR REVIEW

cessed	Review Closed Follow up	Follow up copies Pat Det W.O. SOU Trf CA Media JuvCt Vice Other	Supervisor Approving	Ser No	CC Int

County Attorney

DISMISSED

DAVENPORT POLICE DEPARTMENT
INCIDENT REPORT

0511942		0511942

Beat	Area	Force			Prepared by	Serial Nbr	Initia
2	2B	N	04-17-06 08:10 0874		MORSE	0684	

	Business	Location
ASSAULT INTIMIDATION		3927 WAPELLO AV

Time of Occurrence	MO DA YR	Time	to	MO DA YR	Time	Day of Week	Time of Report	MO DA YR	Time
	06 06 05	11:30		06 06 05	11:30	MONDAY		06 06 05	11:30

Code	Last, First M	S/R	Home Address	DOB	Home Phone
INV	FRY, KENNETH RALPH	M W	0 CITY ST DAVENPORT	01-02-63	940-2180
COM	BRANDLE, CHRISTOPHER J	M W	2111 35TH ST ROCKISLAND	02-24-72	

```
            Officer#   Date       Time
              0684    06-06-05   11:50
                   Media Information
```

On Monday 06-06-05 at approximately 1130 hours, UNIT 101(MORSE) took a disturbance report from 3927 Wapello Avenue, while working the front desk.

Supplement Information

On Monday 06-06-05 at approximately 1130 hours, UNIT 101(MORSE) took a disturbance report from 3917 Wapello Avenue, while working the front desk.

PHONE INTERVIEW WITH COM(CHRIS BRANDLE):

BRANDLE stated he was at his sister's residence, when SUS(KENNETH FRY) barged into the residence and began to swear at the kids and telling them he was going to sue the parents. he then told one of the kids he would shoot him if he did not stay out of the matter. BRANDLE then got into it and told FRY to leave or he was calling the police.

END OF INTERVIEW

I was advised FRY is the land lord and is supposed to be signing the property over to the family. No further action was taken at this time.

MORSE 0684

RECORDS/SUPERVISOR REVIEW

Processed	Review Closed Follow up	Follow up copies Pat Det W.O. SOU Trf CA Media JuvCt Vice Other	Supervisor Approving	Ser No	CC In

ORIGINAL

DAVENPORT POLICE DEPARTMENT
INCIDENT REPORT

0512191

Beat	Area	Force	Date/Time	Prepared by	Serial Nbr	Initial
2	2B		06-14-05 15:19 0667	HAMMES	0660	

Business: HARASSING COMMUNICAT
Location: 3927 WAPELLO AV

Time of Occurrence		Day of Week	Time of Report	
06 06 05 11:00	to 06 09 05 09:37	MONDAY	06 09 05 09:37	

Code	Last, First M	S/R	Home Address	DOB	Home Phone
US	FRY, KENNETH RALPH	M W	1818 MULBERRY AV MUSCATINE	01-02-63	264-8601
OM	MERKS, DIANE MARIE	F W	3927 WAPELLO AV DAVENPORT	01-10-69	940-2180
NV	SHELLABARGER, COLLIN	M W	3927 WAPELLO AV DAVENPORT	01-21-83	940-2180
NV	SHELLABARGER, CRAIG LYNN	M W	3927 WAPELLO AV DAVENPORT	10-06-60	940-2180
NV	GARCIA, KRISTINE	F W	3927 WAPELLO AV DAVENPORT	09-09-89	940-2180

```
Officer#    Date       Time
0660        06-10-05   09:52
0660        06-12-05   15:28
```

Media Information

On 06-09-05 at approximately 0937 hrs Unit 102 (Hammes) and Unit 104 (Jacobsen) were dispatched to 3927 Wapello Avenue reference a disturbance.

Supplement Information

On 06-09-05 at approximately 0937 hrs Unit 102 (Hammes) and Unit 104 (Jacobsen) were dispatched to 3927 Wapello Avenue reference a disturbance. Dispatch advised the Landlord, Kenneth Fry, was threatening to shoot the complainants children.

When we arrived at the residence, we met with Diane Merks. It should be noted that when Merks opened the door to the residence, I could tell she was visibly shaken. Merks voice was trembling and she stated she was scared something bad was going to happen.

*****Interview With Diane Merks*****

According to Merks, she has been having problems with Kenneth Fry. Merks stated Fry owns the residence at 3927 Wapello. Several months ago Fry went to Vietnam, in search of a wife. Merks stated Fry turned the residence over to her and her boyfriend, Craig Shellaberger. Merks stated paper work was drawn up, giving the house to them.

Merks stated when Fry came back from Vietnam, he decided that he wanted his residence back, even though he turned the residence over to her and Shellaberger. Merks stated on 06-06-05 Fry came to the house with an Officer and a Note to Cure was given to her. Fry stated she went to the Court House and was told that her family did not have to move out of the residence.

According to Merks, Fry has been threatening her and her family ever since he served the Note to Cure to her. Merks stated her boyfriend, Craig Shallaberger, received a phone call from Fry. Fry told Craig that he was going to find her (meaning Diane Merks), and him together. Fry then stated he was going to tie him (Craig) up and rape Merks, while Craig watched.

Merks stated Fry also came to the house and threatened her children. Merks stated Fry came into the house and pushed her daughter, Kristine Garcia, and Craig's son, Collin Shallaberger. Fry then told Kristine that he was going to rape her, and then he was going to put her in a pine box. Fry told Collin that he was going to put a bullet in his head.

========================= **County Attorney** =========================

DISMISSED

DAVENPORT POLICE DEPARTMENT
ICIDENT REPORT

According to Merks on today's date, she went outside her residence to leave for work, when she found Fry sitting in his truck. Merks stated when Fry saw her, he left the area. Merks stated she believed that Fry thought she was not home, and that is why he came by the house Merks stated she honestly believes that Fry will harm her children.

Merks stated Fry has been in prison before, for Attempted Murder. According to Merks, Fry is a violent person, and is known to hurt people. Merks stated if Fry is threatening he will carry out his threats. Merks stated Fry is using different vehicle every time he comes to the residence.

*****End Of Interview*****

A report number was given to Merks. She was told to call if she had any other information, or if Fry returned to her residence. Nothing further at this time.

HAMEMS-660

RECORDS/SUPERVISOR REVIEW

rocessed	Review Closed Follow up	Follow up copies Pat Det W.O. SOU Trf CA Media JuvCt Vice Other	Supervisor Approving	Ser No	CC Int
		County Attorney			

DAVENPORT POLICE DEPARTMENT INCIDENT REPORT

FILED 06 FEB -8 PH 2:19
CLERK OF DIST COURT
SCOTT COUNTY, IOWA

0512417

Beat	Area	Force	Date	Time	Serial Nbr	Initial
2	2B	N	06-14-05	15:19 0667	0698	WALKER

Prepared by: WALKER

	Business	Location
SUSPICIOUS		3927 WAPELLO AV

Time of Occurrence	MO DA YR	Time	to	MO DA YR	Time	Day of Week	Time of Report	MO DA YR	Time
	06 11 05	22:55		06 11 05	22:55	SATURDAY		06 12 05	03:19

Code	Last, First M	S/R	Home Address	DOB	Home Phone
NV	GARCIA, CHRISTINE	F W	3927 WAPELLO AV DAVENPORT	09-09-89	563-326-6072
NV	SHELLABARGER, CRAIG LYNN	M W	3927 WAPELLO AV DAVENPORT	10-06-60	563-326-6072
US	FRY, KENNETH RALPH	M W	1818 MULBERRY AV MUSCATINE	01-02-63	
NV	MERKS, DIANE MARIE	F W	3927 WAPELLO AV DAVENPORT	01-10-69	326-6072

Officer# 0698 Date 06-12-05 Time 03:22

Media Information

On Saturday, 6-11-05, at approximately 2255 hours Units were dispatched to 3729 Wapello Ave. in reference to suspicious activity.

Supplement Information

On Saturday, 6-11-05, at approximately 2255 hours Unit 303 (L. Walker) and Unit 309 (Miller) were dispatched to 3729 Wapello Ave., in reference to suspicious activity. Upon arrival I spoke with Diane Merks.

INTERVIEW WITH DIANE MERKS:

Merks told me she has been having problems with Kenneth Fry, a white male, approximately 45 years old. She said she bought the house from him and two vehicles. Merks told me Fry has "lost his mind" and has been threatening to harm her and her children. Merks told me her daughter called her tonight and said there was someone pounding on the back door. She said her daughters were home alone and scared to look out the door to see who was pounding. Merks told me she told her daughter to call the police just in case it was Fry at the back door.

Merks told me Fry is staying with his brother at 1818 Mulberry Ave., in Muscatine. She said Fry is taking her to small claims court on Tuesday, 6-14-05, at 1:00PM in reference to the house.

Merks told me she tried to get a restraining order against Fry for his threats to harm her and her children but she was denied.

END OF INTERVIEW WITH DIANE MERKS.

See additional supplements for further.
L. Walker 698

RECORDS/SUPERVISOR REVIEW

Processed	Review Closed Follow up	Follow up copies Pat Det W.O. SOU Trf CA Media JuvCt Vice Other	Supervisor Approving	Ser No	CC Int
			County Attorney		

DISMISSED

DAVENPORT POLICE DEPARTMENT INCIDENT REPORT

0512417

Beat	Area	Force	Date	Time		Prepared by	Serial Nbr	Initial
2	2B	N	06-14-05	15:19	0667	MILLER	0738	

	Business	Location
SUSPICIOUS		3927 WAPELLO AV

Time of occurrence	MO DA YR	Time	to	MO DA YR	Time	Day of Week	Time of Report	MO DA YR	Time
	06 11 05	22:55		06 11 05	22:55	SATURDAY		06 12 05	03:19

Code	Last, First M	S/R	Home Address	DOB	Home Phone
VV	GARCIA, CHRISTINE	F W	3927 WAPELLO AV DAVENPORT	09-09-89	563-326-6072
VV	SHELLABARGER, CRAIG LYNN	M W	3927 WAPELLO AV DAVENPORT	10-06-60	563-326-6072
IS	FRY, KENNETH RALPH	M W	1818 MULBERRY AV MUSCATINE	01-02-63	

```
Officer#   Date      Time
  0738    06-12-05  03:23
  0738    06-12-05  03:38
```

Supplement Information

On Saturday June 11, 2005 at 2255 hours Units 309 (Miller) and 303 (Walker) responded to 3927 Wapello Av reference suspicious activity.

Upon arrival we met with Craig Shellabarger and Diane Maks. Ofc. Bruns spoke with Diane and I spoke with Craig.

INTEVIEW WITH CRAIG SHELLABARGER

Craig stated his daughter Christine called him and Diane saying Kenneth was there trying to get in the house. He described Kenneth as a white male about 5'8" and weighed about 260 lbs. He said he was born in 1963. Craig also said his name was Kenneth Fry and that he lived in Muscatine. Craig commented that Kenneth only comes around when he is not there.

Craig complained that Kenneth stole his corvette a while back and was storing it in a storage shed.

END OF INTERVIEW WITH CRAIG SHELLABARGER

Next I spoke with Christine Garcia.

INTEVIEW WITH CHRISTINE GARCIA

Christine said she heard a car pull up and some noises on the porch. She didn't think anything of it because she thought Diane and Craig were just coming home. When no one came in the house she looked out the blinds and saw Kenneth walking around on the gravel. He saw her as she was closing the blinds and yelled "Hey wait a minute, open the door." Christine said she went into grab her sister and they hid in her bedroom with a baseball bat and called the police. Christine said Kenneth was there for about 10 minutes before he may have left. She said she heard him come but didn't hear him go.

END OF INTERVIEW WITH CHRISTINE GARCIA

Muscatine County and The Muscatine Police Department were notified of Kenneth being an officer safety issue due to him being a felon and carrying weapons.

Nothing further at this time.

Miller #738

RECORDS/SUPERVISOR REVIEW

Processed	Review Closed Follow up	Follow up copies Pat Det W.O. SOU Trf CA Media JuvCt Vice Other	Supervisor Approving	Ser No	CC Int

County Attorney

KENNETH RALPH FRY

IN THE IOWA DISTRICT COURT FOR SCOTT COUNTY

Agency **DAP**   Report # **0512191**   **ADULT**

Criminal No. **FECR 279164**

THE STATE OF IOWA

COMPLAINT AND AFFIDAVIT

VS.   Co-Defendants: No   Printed: 06-14-05 15:06:24

FRY, KENNETH RALPH   DOB **01-02-1963**   SS# **481-85-6186**

Address **1818 MULBERRY AV MUSCATINE IA**

The defendant is accused of the crimes below charged in that the Defendant did

COUNT I
on or about the 06th day of **June**, 2005 (at approximately 11:00 o'clock **am**) at **3927 WAPELLO AV DAVENPORT**, in Scott County, Iowa commit the crime of **BURGLARY 2ND DEGREE** in violation of Section **713.5** of the current Code of Iowa.

COUNT II
on or about the 06th day of **June**, 2005 (at approximately 11:00 o'clock **am**) at **3927 WAPELLO AV DAVENPORT**, in Scott County, Iowa commit the crime of **THEFT 2ND DEGREE** in violation of Section **714.2(2)** of the current Code of Iowa.

COUNT III
on or about the 06th day of **June**, 2005 (at approximately 11:00 o'clock **am**) at **3927 WAPELLO AV DAVENPORT**, in Scott County, Iowa commit the crime of **FORGERY (CLASS D FELONY)** in violation of Section **715A.2(2A)** of the current Code of Iowa.

COUNT IV
on or about the 06th day of **June**, 2005 (at approximately 11:00 o'clock **am**) at **3927 WAPELLO AV DAVENPORT**, in Scott County, Iowa commit the crime of **HARASSMENT 1ST DEGREE** in violation of Section **708.7(2)** of the current Code of Iowa.

COUNT V
on or about the 06th day of **June**, 2005 (at approximately 11:00 o'clock **am**) at **3927 WAPELLO AV DAVENPORT**, in Scott County, Iowa commit the crime of **STALKING 1ST OFFENSE** in violation of Section **708.11(3)(C)** of the current Code of Iowa.

COMPLAINANT _____

STATE OF IOWA, County of Scott ss:

AFFIDAVIT

I, the undersigned state that the following facts known by me or told to me by other reliable persons form the basis for my belief that the Defendant committed these crimes.

During a period between June 2 and June 11, 2005 Officers responded to 3927 Wapello Av reference on-going harassment.

The defendant, KENNETH RALPH FRY is being charged with the above crimes as a result of the following information.

On June 1, 2005 the defendant sold a vehicle to the victim for cash money and signed the title and provided a bill of sale. Two days later the defendant took the vehicle and requested a new title from the state claiming the original had been stolen.

On June 6, 2005 the defendant telephoned the victim and threatened to commit a sexual assault. The defendant then drove to the victims house, forced his way into the house and assaulted a resident. The defendant then repeated his threat to commit a sexual assault and threatened to shoot another resident of the home.

On multiple occasions following these incidents the defendant was observed sitting in his vehicle outside the victims house.

DEFENDANTS COPY

DISMISSED

DAVENPORT POLICE DEPARTMENT
INCIDENT REPORT

0517408							0517408	
Beat	Area	Force	01-24-06 10:33 0825			Prepared by	Serial Nbr	Initial
2	2B	N				MEYRER	0567	
	CRT ORDER		Business			Location 3706 S CONCORD ST		
Time of Occurrence	MO DA YR	Time	MO DA YR	Time	Day of Week	Time of Report	MO DA YR	Time
	08 04 05	13:30	08 04 05	13:30	THURSDAY		08 04 05	19:13

Code	Last, First M	S/R	Home Address	DOB	Home Phone
SUS	FRY, KENNETH RALPH	M W	1818 MULBERRY ST MUSCATINE	01-02-63	271-9537
COM	MERKS, DIANE MARIE	F W	3706 S CONCORD ST DAVENPORT	01-10-69	271-9537
WIT	GARCIA, KRISTINE	F W	3709 S CONCORD ST DAVENPORT	09-09-89	

```
         Officer#    Date       Time
          0567     08-04-05    20:55
```

Media Information

On August 4th at 1913 hours unit # 202 Meyrer responded to 3709 S Concord in reference to violation of a domestic order.

Supplement Information

On August 4th at 1913 hours unit # 202 Meyrer responded to 3709 S Concord St. in reference to a violation of a domestic order. When I arrived I met with Diane Merks who stated the following.

Interview with Diane Merks:

Diane said she currently has an active restraining order against Kenneth Fry. Today Diane was gone from the home most of the day. Diane's daughter Kristine Garcia was home alone. At 1330 hours Kristine observed the suspect Kenneth Fry knocking at the rear door. Kristine would not answer the door. Kenneth then tried the door however it was locked.

Interview with Kristine Garcia:

Kristine said at 1330 hours Kenneth Fry was knocking at the rear door of the home. Kristine would not answer the door. Kenneth did try the door to see if it was locked. Kristine was asked if she actually seen Kenneth do this. Kristine said she did see Kenneth at the rear door.

Kristine could not call the police as they do not have a house phone. This is why the police was called at a later time.

A warrant request is being made for the arrest of Kenneth Fry for violating the protection order.

Nothing further at this time.

Meyrer 567

RECORDS/SUPERVISOR REVIEW

Processed	Review Closed Follow up	Follow up copies Pat Det W.O. SOU Trf CA Media JuvCt Vice Other	Supervisor Approving	Ser No	CC Int

ORIGINAL

0517408	DAVENPORT POLICE DEPARTMENT INCIDENT REPORT			0517408	
Beat 2	Area 2B	Force N	01-24-06 10:33 0825	Prepared by DENGER	Serial Nbr 0667	Initial
CRT ORDER			Business	Location 3706 S CONCORD ST	
Time of Occurrence	MO DA YR 08 04 05	Time 13:30	to MO DA YR 08 04 05 Time 13:30 Day of Week THURSDAY	Time of Report	MO DA YR 08 04 05	Time 19:13
Code	Last, First M		S/R Home Address		DOB	Home Phone
SUS	FRY, KENNETH RALPH		M W 1818 MULBERRY ST MUSCATINE		01-02-63	271-9537

Officer#   Date   Time
0667   08-16-05   09:24

Supplement Information

On Tuesday August 16, 2005 at approximately 0925 hrs I telephoned (563-732-4105) Plasticraft Mfg to verify Kenneth Fry's employment.

I spoke with Michelle Williams who identified herself as the person in charge. Williams said Kenneth Fry does work at Plasticraft and was working on Thursday August 4, 2005. She said Fry clocked in at 1306 hrs and clocked out at 2305 hrs.

Plasticraft is located in Wilton, Iowa approximately 25-30 miles from Davenport.

Det Denger
0667

DISMISSED

Trial Case Details Filings

Filings
Title: STATE VS FRY, KENNETH RALPH
Case: 07821 FECR279164 (SCOTT)

Event	Filed By	Filed	Create Date	Last Updated
CCU SENT		11/25/2005	11/25/2005	11/25/2005
COMPUTER GENERATED NOTICE		10/25/2005	10/25/2005	10/25/2005
Comments: FINAL CCU NOTICE				
INDIGENT DEFENSE CLAIM FORM	STATE PUBLIC DEFENDERS OFFICE	10/21/2005	10/24/2005	10/24/2005
Comments: $125.00 ATTY MOLYNEAUX				
NO CONTACT ORDER	SIVRIGHT DAVID	08/17/2005	08/17/2005	08/17/2005
Comments: CASE DISMISSED				
ORDER OF DISPOSITION	SIVRIGHT DAVID	08/16/2005	08/17/2005	08/17/2005
Comments: CASE DISMISSED; COSTS TAXED TO STATE				
MOTION	CUSACK ROBERT L	08/16/2005	08/17/2005	08/17/2005
Comments: TO DISMISS				
ORDER FOR PRETRIAL CONFERENCE	SMITH MARK J	08/12/2005	08/16/2005	08/16/2005
Comments: PTC CON'T 8/26/05 1:00				
VICTIM IMPACT STATEMENT		08/11/2005	08/12/2005	08/12/2005
Comments: DOES WISH TO REGISTER				
VICTIM IMPACT STATEMENT		08/11/2005	08/12/2005	08/12/2005
Comments: DOES WISH TO REGISTER				
VICTIM IMPACT STATEMENT		08/11/2005	08/12/2005	08/12/2005
Comments: DOES WISH TO REGISTER				
WAIVER OF SPEEDY TRIAL		07/21/2005	07/22/2005	07/22/2005
ORDER FOR PRETRIAL CONFERENCE	PELTON CHARLES H	07/21/2005	07/21/2005	07/21/2005
Comments: 08/12/05 1:00; DEFT ARRAIGNED; PLEADS NOT				

http://www.iowacourts.state.ia.us/ESAWebApp/TViewFilings   3/22/06

Made in the USA